Charles Wesley

Worship Feast

12 Worship Services Based on Wesley's Hymns

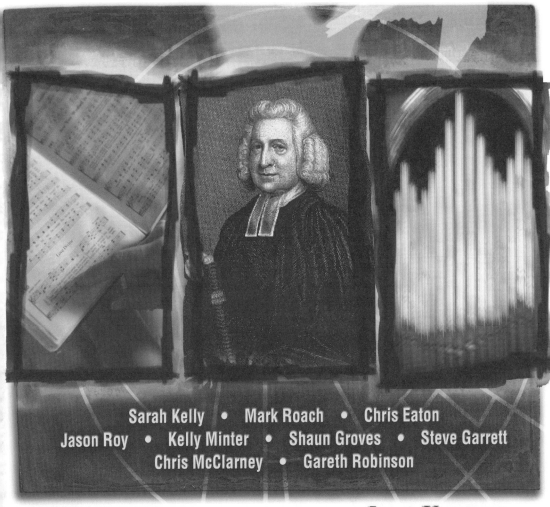

Sarah Kelly • Mark Roach • Chris Eaton
Jason Roy • Kelly Minter • Shaun Groves • Steve Garrett
Chris McClarney • Gareth Robinson

Jenny Youngman

Abingdon Press
Nashville

MANUFACTURED IN THE UNITED STATES OF AMERICA

08 09 10 11 12 13 14 15 17 18—10 9 8 7 6 5 4 3 2 1

COVER DESIGN: KEELY MOORE

Contents

Meet the Writer

Jenny Youngman has worked and worshiped with youth for ten years. She is the creator of the WORSHIP FEAST series for youth groups, and she is passionate about creative worship. Jenny leads workshops and worship gatherings for youth retreats and youth worker events. She lives with her family outside of Nashville, TN.

The Wesleys

The Original Caped Crusaders

Growing up in a Christian home with strong links to The United Methodist Church, I've always been fascinated by John and Charles Wesley. Truly they are the original dynamic duo! Imagining them riding horseback around the country preaching and writing songs always conjured up vivid pictures in my young mind of what people look like who are totally "sold out" for God.

The England in which the Wesleys were born and raised was dark, lawless, and for the most part debauched. While at Oxford University, they formed a small group called "The Holy Club" or the "Methodists." The members of this group dedicated their lives to purity, God's Word, fasting, praying, and visiting the poor and needy—all of which served as a great foundation for their future.

Picture this: For nearly fifty years, John rode around on a horse, preaching up to three sermons a day, speaking to thousands of people about Christ and calling them to repentance. And then there was Charles, who wrote over six thousand songs, many of which form the basis of our worship today—and he is still considered one of the church's greatest hymn writers!

The impact both Wesley's have had is immense because of their willingness to let God use them in whatever way God wanted. By the end of their lives, England was a different place, thanks largely to their efforts in turning a nation towards God.

I hope that through these new melodies set to Charles Wesley hymns, people will, in some small way, catch a glimpse of the great God that this "Dynamic Duo" loved and served faithfully.

—John Hartley

How to Use Worship Feast Charles Wesley

This project came about when John Hartley came to us at Abingdon Youth with a CD he was producing. The record was to be a collection of Charles Wesley hymns set to new melodies and sung by some of today's most listened-to Christian artists and worship leaders. Immediately we thought of pairing the CD with a WORSHIP FEAST resource in the hopes of young people learning to worship through classic Wesley lyrics. We dreamed of a new generation of youth who would find the hope, the truth, and the love of God in Wesley's beautiful poetry.

The dream is reality: The album *Love Divine* is finished, and you are holding a new WORSHIP FEAST resource that includes reflections from each of the artists on the record. The artists look back on their experiences with the hymns and give us a little insight about how Wesley's words inspired them to a deeper faith. Also included with each reflection is a worship meditation for use with your students. Each meditation offers a Scripture focus, a creative worship experience, and an emphasis on learning the accompanying song. Of course we hope the songs find their way into your regular worship times— and these meditations are a way to help the youth learn the songs and make that happen.

It is our prayer that through these lyrics and melodies, your youth will develop a heart to praise God!

Seriously. . . Directions for Singing?

John and Charles Wesley did not take lightly the business of hymns. In fact, they took hymns very, very seriously. Not only were they prolific and prophetic in their lyricism, but also they were intense about how and when the lyrics were to be sung. See John's "Directions for Singing" on the next page.

On one hand you say: "Yes! Believers should gather together and sing with all their hearts. They should take in these great lyrics and let the Spirit of God cover them." On the other hand you say, "Geez! Relax Wesleys; not everyone has such a grasp on hymnody or on singing in general for that matter."

In any case, the "Directions for Singing" from *John Wesley's Select Hymns* may help us to take our singing in worship a little more seriously. Sure, it may sound a little over the top, but note especially number 7: "Above all sing spiritually. Have an eye to God in every word you sing." Whether we're singing classic hymns set to classic melodies, or ancient words set to new tunes, or altogether contemporary songs, let us sing spiritually and have an eye to God in every word. Let us not sing as though we were half-dead or bawl so as to steal the show!

I'm not quite sure how to apply numbers 1 and 2, but it is my prayer that a rising generation of believers would learn to sing and worship with all their hearts, that they would sing classic songs and new songs, and that they would participate fully in the worship of their amazing, awe-inspiring Creator. May it be so!

Directions for Singing

1. Learn these tunes before you learn any others; afterwards learn as many as you please.

2. Sing them exactly as they are printed here, without altering or mending them at all; and if you have learned to sing them otherwise, unlearn it as soon as you can.

3. Sing all. See that you join with the congregation as frequently as you can. Let not a slight degree of weakness or weariness hinder you. If it is a cross to you, take it up, and you will find it a blessing.

4. Sing lustily and with good courage. Beware of singing as if you were half dead, or half asleep; but lift up your voice with strength. Be no more afraid of your voice now, nor more ashamed of its being heard, than when you sung the songs of Satan.

5. Sing modestly. Do not bawl, so as to be heard above or distinct from the rest of the congregation, that you may not destroy the harmony; but strive to unite your voices together, so as to make one clear melodious sound.

6. Sing in time. Whatever time is sung be sure to keep with it. Do not run before nor stay behind it; but attend close to the leading voices, and move therewith as exactly as you can; and take care not to sing too slow. This drawling way naturally steals on all who are lazy; and it is high time to drive it out from us, and sing all our tunes just as quick as we did at first.

7. Above all sing spiritually. Have an eye to God in every word you sing. Aim at pleasing him more than yourself, or any other creature. In order to do this attend strictly to the sense of what you sing, and see that your heart is not carried away with the sound, but offered to God continually; so shall your singing be such as the Lord will approve here, and reward you when he cometh in the clouds of heaven.

—From *John Wesley's Select Hymns,* 1761

Above all sing
spiritually. Have an
eye to God
in every word you
sing. Aim at
pleasing him
more than yourself,
or any other
creature.

Reflections
&
Worship
Meditations

O For a Thousand Tongues to Sing

by Chris McClarney

I need an extra arm. I realize that this is a strange way to start a reflection about a hymn, but follow me ...

You see, I drive a German-made car, circa 1988. It has a manual transmission, and if you are one of the many blessed individuals who has had the privilege of owning a quality, "vintage," European vehicle with a manual transmission, then you know that despite its superior craftsmanship and exceptional good looks, it has an irritating design flaw—one that the rest of the world seemed to catch onto long before 1988—and one that bugs me almost every day, making me wish I had an extra arm to compensate: There are no cup holders!

Before you give me the speech about how I shouldn't be eating and drinking while driving anyway, let me explain further. I don't need cup holders so that I can drink in the car. I just want to transport my daily coffee from Starbucks to my office without scalding my inner thighs. I don't even want to talk about the times I've tried to grab a latté for a friend, too—Ouch!

Three arms. Problem solved! One to steer, one to shift, and one to hold my macciatto. (Now, how to call the office and let them know I'm running late ... that's something else.)

Perhaps you've never wished for an extra arm (I realize it would be hard to shop for T-shirts), but have you ever wished you were a little stronger? wiser? faster? The world is becoming busier and busier. Modern life is pushing us to accomplish more ... do a better job ... be a better person. When faced with those daunting tasks, I need caffeine—and look at me—I can't even do that right.

The truth is that there are only so many hours in a day and only so many things one individual can accomplish within that allotted time. Even as I'm typing this, I can hear one of my daughters in the next room, and I am torn between finishing my thoughts or playing.

OK, I'm back now. (And I'm covered in princess stickers. Don't ask.) The point is, at the moment, we are limited beings in a limited world.

God, on the other hand, is immeasurable, infinite, indescribable, and never-ending. God is entirely too complex for even the wisest to comprehend—able to be all places at all times and limited by nothing. Yet God extended to us, the limited ones, an invitation to be in relationship.

Therein lies the rub. One of the keys to a quality relationship is give and take. If I just took and took and never offered of myself, then I probably wouldn't have very many friends to whom I could deliver leg-burning coffee.

But what do I have to give back to God? God has given so much, expecting

nothing in return. I am hopeless in my own strength to ever adequately reciprocate that kind of love!

It was with this revelation of inadequacy, specifically the deficiency of the contents of his own mouth, that Peter Böhler said to his friend Charles Wesley—"Had I a thousand tongues, I would praise Him with them all" —a thought that Charles would later use in a poem. The poem has since become an anthem.

> "O for a thousand tongues to sing
>   my great Redeemer's praise!
> the glories of my God and King,
>   the triumphs of His grace!"

O Lord, if I just had 999 more ways to say thank you, 999 more ways to lift you up. If only I had 999 more tongues to say "I love you, too."

Originally written for "The Anniversary Day of One's Conversion," the song is a reminder to all believers of God's grace and a call to daily lay down our personal riches for the One who laid down all authority and power to have a relationship with us. It is a song of rededication, both a reminder of where we've come from as well as a standard by which to move forward.

And because I know you are wondering . . . if for some reason I did have three arms, I would use them all to praise my Lord.

To hear more of Chris's music, visit www.myspace.com/gracecenter.

Worship Meditation: O For a Thousand Tongues

Scripture: *"About midnight Paul and Silas were praying and singing hymns to God, and the prisoners were listening to them. Suddenly there was an earthquake, so violent that the foundations of the prison were shaken; and immediately all the doors were opened and everyone's chains were unfastened"* (Acts 16:25).

Opening Prayer: "God, we pray that you would hear our worship as though we each had one thousand tongues to sing your praise. Receive our singing, our prayers, and our worship—and let your glory fill this place. Amen."

Read the Scripture: Invite someone to read aloud **Acts 16:16-40**. Then reread verse 25 for emphasis.

Creative Worship: Cover a wall with mural paper and set out paints and paint brushes. Invite youth to draw images that portray worshiping God with "one thousand tongues." Remind youth that, while in prison, Paul and Silas worshiped in song, and their song brought freedom to those around them. Suggest they think about that sort of unabashed worship as they paint.

Closing: Sing together "O For a Thousand Tongues" from the *Love Divine* CD.

I Know That My Redeemer Lives

by Steve Garrett

I feel like I just met Charles Wesley for the first time. Not too long ago I headed into the studio to record a lesser-known tune of his titled "I Know That My Redeemer Lives," and to my surprise, there he was. I think I had imagined him to be a stodgy, wig-wearing, eighteenth-century hymn-writer with dusty theology. Instead I discovered a preacher and a poet whose deep conviction and musical artistry have refreshing relevance for the twenty-first century.

No doubt the modern musical interpretation of this hymn helped grease the wheels for my newfound relationship with the past. But, in any case, as a pastor and singer-songwriter myself, I am glad to have found a new hero possessing a singable theology and the ability to create timeless art.

As the son of a preacher, I have long been familiar with his perennial hits like "Christ the Lord Is Risen Today," "And Can It Be," and "Hark! the Herald Angels Sing." But now these songs have taken on greater significance. I have been motivated to dig a bit deeper into the life of this great figure who at times has stood in the historical shadow of his brother John Wesley. This, of course, is understandable considering the profound and lasting impact of John's life and ministry on saints and sinners alike. But the fruit of Charles' life seems no less impressive to me.

While reading portions of *The Journal of Charles Wesley*, I paid particular interest to entries he made in 1741, just prior to writing "I Know That My Redeemer Lives." On Tuesday, April 21, 1741, he specifically refers to a homily he delivered at the funeral of "sister Richardson," with the text being taken from **Job 19:25**. Wesley recounts the worshipful atmosphere in the crowded room with such joyful and hopeful terms that I can't help but think this event could have been the initial seeds of inspiration for this powerful hymn. One of the stanzas in particular seems to reflect this atypical funeral scene:

> "Joyful in hope, my spirit soars
>   To meet thee from above
> Thy goodness thankfully adores
>   And sure I taste thy love."

In his journal entry, Wesley goes on to describe the opposition they faced on the street as they left the funeral service and made their way to the interment site: "The whole Society followed her to her grave. Through all the city Satan raged exceedingly in his children, who threw dirt and stones at us . . . ."* The persecution and heckling would not deter their worship. Clearly they were "joyful in hope."

This looks like authentic worship to me—a wonderful intersection of Scripture and human experience. After all, worship is, in many ways, our heartfelt response to God revealing more of himself to us. I am reminded of

the apostle John's words: "We love because he first loved us" (1 John 4:19).

Charles Wesley had a rare ability to transform deep biblical truth into poetry. And with evangelistic fervor, he and his brother John most effectively employed both sermon and song in the proclamation of the gospel of Jesus Christ. Wesley's journal subtly reveals a man fueled by prayer and motivated by a great love for God's presence. Even with his grueling travel and preaching schedule (sometimes 4 to 5 times a day), he found time to write his hymns of praise, totaling thousands by the end of his life. A movement had begun and the church began to grow.

My chance meeting with Charles Wesley has stirred within me a greater desire to keep Jesus at the center of all I say and do. Like Wesley, I long to preach with greater conviction, widely proclaim the love of God, and be creative even in adversity. I want to worship with greater passion. If only I had a thousand tongues!

* *The Journal of Charles Wesley.* Copyright © 1999 by the Wesley Center for Applied Theology. Scanned and edited by Ryan Danker. Used by permission.

*To *hear more of Steve's music,* visit* *www.stevegarrett.net.*

Worship Meditation: I Know That My Redeemer Lives

Scripture: *"For I know that my Redeemer lives, and that at the last he will stand upon the earth; and after my skin has been thus destroyed, then in my flesh I shall see God, whom I shall see on my side, and my eyes shall behold, and not another"* (Job 19:25-27).

Opening Prayer: Read the following prayer: "Redeemer God, we come before you with joyful hope. We know that, no matter the pit in which we find ourselves, we can declare, like Job, that our Redeemer lives and cares for us. Receive our worship and show us your glory. Amen."

Read the Scripture: Assign the verses from **Job 19** to several readers. Explain that Job is known for remaining faithful despite suffering extreme hardship. Encourage them to read with passion as though they can feel Job's pain. Then reread verses 25–27 for emphasis.

Creative Worship: Set out several magazines and newspapers, posterboard, scissors, and glue. Encourage students to create a collage that illustrates **Job 19**. As background music, play "I Know That My Redeemer Lives" from the *Love Divine* CD.

Closing: Sing together "I Know That My Redeemer Lives" from the *Love Divine* CD. Pray that your students will declare from the pit of despair that they have a Redeemer who is always with them.

Come Thou Long Expected Jesus

by Gareth Robinson

I have to be honest—I've always been nervous about hymns that have been updated with a new melody. I grew up with a certain love and appreciation of the musicality and time-honored nature of the hymns we sing in church. Too often I've thought that the new tunes didn't really add anything to the song. But as time passed, I discovered that not everybody sang the same tune to the same hymn; this fact hit me hard when I moved to America. Suddenly I had no choice but to sing new tunes to my old favorites; and I slowly became more receptive to the idea of different tunes to the same words.

However, when John Hartley, Chris Eaton, and I sat down to write new tunes to Wesley's words, I was determined to stay away from his better-known hymns. Clearly my preferences were still influencing me and, when "Come Thou Long Expected Jesus" was suggested, I was not convinced. How can you bring something new to such a powerful hymn? So I was thrilled, humbled, and a little amazed that what we tried worked—we created a tune that grabs the energy of the words and shouts the joy we have in Immanuel, God with us!

Advent has always been a special time for me. At the church where I grew up, every week through the four weekends of Advent, we would light a new candle on the Advent wreath to mark the preparation for Christmas—and those days were always filled with excitement and anticipation. To me, this hymn captures the sense of the season better than any other Advent hymn: the sense of the now-but-not-yet, the promise of Christ's return, and the recognition of his grace that gathers us into the story.

> "Come, thou long-expected Jesus,
>   born to set thy people free;
> From our fears and sins release us,
>   let us find our rest in Thee."

Advent is a time to not only prepare ourselves for Christmas but also to remember that we live in expectation of Jesus' imminent return—hence the first line. His return has been expected for a long time. I sometimes wonder at the apostle Paul's words when he speaks of Christ's return as imminent, thinking, *Lord, is this really possible?* But then I look around at the world and see the mess we're in, and I think, *Yes, so much around us confirms that darkness is in a cosmic battle with light, and my hope is set on this light winning—with people being set free, released from fears and sins, and finding rest in God alone.* Surely today we are one step closer to the fulfillment of the ages, the culmination of Scripture, and the return of our King.

Jesus' kingdom reign is both now—but not yet. Many great theologians have written about this fact; Jesus taught us to pray "your kingdom come," since he knew we would need to keep on praying it throughout our lifetime.

The now-but-not-yet continues in verse 2. Verse 1 sets us up with the

expectation of the Kingdom—freedom from sin and fear, rest in God, strength, hope, and fulfillment of desire and joy. Verse 2 cries out "let it be!" Jesus, do the Moses thing and get us out of this mess!

It's no small thing that Charles writes "born to reign in us" rather than "over us." Jesus reigns in us: That means the Kingdom is right here, my heart is his throne, my body is his temple, and we are the bearers of the King. The Kingdom, as described in verse 1, could break out at any moment, because the King is right here! So bring your kingdom now, Lord, through me. Let me bring others your peace, forgiveness, strength, and joy.

And, as if Wesley hasn't packed enough theology into this short hymn, he can't conclude without reminding us that it's all grace. It's because Jesus is worthy, not because we are. It's because of the Father's grace, not our goodness, that we get to join in with living this kingdom life. We might be co-heirs with Christ, but let's not kid ourselves that it's because of us. This kingdom is one of grace, initiated and completed by the Lord—but what amazing grace it is!

There really isn't any other response. My dictionary says that the word *rejoice* means to "feel or show great joy or delight." We're full of joy because of the kingdom we live in now, because the Lord will wrap up time into eternity and bring about the peace we all desire, and because he is here with us. It's true—I love this hymn!

**To hear more of Gareth's music, visit
www.garethrobinson.net.*

Worship Meditation: Come Thou Long Expected Jesus

Scripture: *"I'm baptizing you here in the river, turning your old life in for a kingdom life. The real action comes next: The main character in this drama—compared to him I'm a mere stagehand—will ignite the kingdom life within you, a fire within you, the Holy Spirit within you, changing you from the inside out"* (Matthew 3:11, THE MESSAGE).

Opening Prayer: "Come, long-expected Jesus and rule in our hearts. Release us from our fears and our sins and be our hope. Bring your kingdom in us. Amen."

Read the Scripture: Ask for a volunteer to read aloud **Matthew 3:11-12** from *THE MESSAGE*.

Creative Worship: Set out a pillar candle for each of your youth. Say: "Each of you has a candle representing the potential for "a fire within you" for God's kingdom. As we sing, when you feel so moved, go and light your candle as a prayer for the long-expected Jesus to rule in your heart and ignite the "kingdom life within you." Play or sing together "Come Thou Long Expected Jesus" from the *Love Divine* CD.

Closing: Raise up your hands as you cry out, "Come into our world, long-expected Jesus!"

Love Divine

by Sarah Kelly

I grew up in the "passion" generation. Modern worship is my life; so when I was asked to participate in this project, I must admit, I had no idea of the spiritual growth I would experience. Sitting in the studio and singing "Love Divine" for the first time, my eyes teared up and my heartbeat quickened. The lyrics—so personal, introspective, and prayerful—spoke of a God who I am just beginning to know. It was like I was opening Charles Wesley's journal and reading his most personal thoughts, written to his most trusted confidant—Jesus Christ. Suddenly the words, "I love you, I need you" from my favorite, modern worship songs just didn't seem as deep of a cry when hearing these lyrics drenched in thought and meaning. I love the simplicity of modern worship music, but there is definitely something in these words that we have forgotten in our pursuit to bring new songs into the church.

I love that Wesley's songs seem to look forward to heaven. I love that his goal wasn't a comfortable life but a glorious heaven.

> "Changed from glory into glory,
>   till in heaven we take our place,
> Till we cast our crowns before thee,
>   lost in wonder, love, and praise."

Now that's someone who had a vision of heaven!

Don't you wish we could sit down with Wesley and hear the full stories behind these songs? As a songwriter I know that it takes a lot of emotion and difficult circumstance for such intense word and melody to move from deep within to the outside world. I am so grateful that he left us these songs as a hug for the hard times as well as a reminder to anticipate what lies ahead for the faithful! It is as if Wesley is our "great great great grandpa" in the faith, and he left us his music to run to when we need to remember where we come from and what is truly important.

There are no "filler" words in Wesley's works, just lyrics you could think about for weeks and then only *begin* to fully comprehend. That fact has challenged my personal writing as well, giving me permission to explore "outside of the lines" of modern worship.

So on this journey that has led you to stumble upon these older hymns, may the love of God guide you, may God's faithfulness always amaze you, and may Charles Wesley's words deepen your love for the Lord, as they have done for me!

To hear more of Sarah's music, visit www.sarahkelly.com.

Worship Meditation: Love Divine

Scripture: *"For God so loved the world that he gave his only Son, so that everyone who believes in him may not perish but may have eternal life"* (John 3:16).

Opening Prayer: "Lord, we are so amazed that you would come from heaven to take our place. Receive our praise as we lift you up and sing of your love that excels all other loves. Amen."

Read the Scripture: Ask for a volunteer to read aloud John 3:16.

Creative Worship: The new arrangement of "Love Divine" from the CD *Love Divine* lends itself well to liturgical dance. Allow time for your worship band to learn the song and ask the rest of your group to choreograph a liturgical dance and then present it as an act of worship. If you have any anti-dancers, ask them to participate as Scripture readers or pray-ers. If possible, present this entire meditation in your church's worship service.

Closing: Pray this prayer or one of your own: "Lord, we are thankful that you loved us so much that you would come down to earth and meet us where we are. Fix us, bless us, change us from glory into glory until we take our place in heaven. Amen."

And Can It Be

by Jason Roy

What does it feel like to know beyond a shadow of a doubt that you are guilty—that no person, no circumstance, no help of any kind can ransom you from the hand of judgment? Surely a feeling of hopelessness envelops anyone in that situation. And then the moment comes when, in brilliance, the light flashes on and you discover that, for no apparent reason at all, except love, of course, Jesus steps between you and eternal consequence—and you are saved.

That is the paradox, isn't it? A woefully sinful people inhabiting an earth that is no longer Eden; and yet love finds a way, reaching through all space and time to exhibit extraordinary qualities: forgiveness, forgetfulness, self-sacrifice, and ultimately restoration.

Isn't it just like our God to paint a picture of love that is unbelievably hard to live up to? Isn't it just like our King to show the ultimate love every single moment of our lives? Not just in a moment of kindness, but in every moment—when things have gone terribly awry—when sickness invades our lives, when tragedy has stolen our peace, and when everything we believed to be certain is gone. Still there is God's amazing love.

Reflection

This truth illuminates a startling contrast between what *we* call love and what God shows us *is* love every single day. Suddenly "I love you" means a whole lot more than how we use the words. Charles Wesley completely understood that truth when he wrote this song. Our love is at best weak when compared to the love of God, our Creator.

Upon listening to this song, I often ask myself: *With whom have I shared such a reprieving love? To whom have I given pardon when they were dead wrong? To whom have I shown the love of Christ in the past few days, months, or even years?* That brings me to my next questions: Whom have you loved? And whom have you not loved well? Those questions may send you on a journey, and if they do, my prayer is that you would be willing to face the cold, hard reality of your personal lacking with a resolve that says, "I'm going to get to the bottom of this."

As I journey through my encounters with those I say that I love, I am hit with feelings of remorse over my choices in the heat of the moment. Even as I type these words, my mind is remembering the past two days and how quickly I became angry and judgmental toward my wife and my children. It's not like I'm a bad person ... or is it? It's not like I'm a sinner ... or is it? Yes, we all are sinners, but by grace we are saved from a sentence of death, and as we show grace, we show ourselves to be true followers of Christ who possess a more complete knowledge of the love of Jesus. So let your heart be troubled—even let your heart hurt—for in your weakness, you are made perfect in his strength. Turn your eyes upon Jesus and refocus your love and affection for those around you. Remember the amazing love that you are so blessed to experience and then share that gift with everyone you know.

> "Amazing love, how can it be
> that thou, my God, shouldst die for me?"

Let's allow amazing love to be the rule by which we live our lives every day.

To hear more of Jason's music, visit www.myspace.com/jasonkroy.

Worship Meditation: And Can It Be

Scripture: *"There is therefore now no condemnation for those who are in Christ Jesus"* (Romans 8:1).

Opening Prayer: "God, we cannot fathom that you would stoop down to know us and to free us from our sins. We are amazed at the love you have for us. Fill us with that love and mercy, immense and free. Amen."

Read the Scripture: Ask for volunteers to read aloud **Romans 8:1**. Talk for a minute about the idea that we don't have to dread or fear condemnation—that in Christ, we are free from our sin. Encourage students to talk through what they believe that truth means and what it means for them personally.

Creative Worship: Sing together the song "And Can It Be" from the *Love Divine* CD. Then design "No Condemnation" T-shirts. Hand out solid-color T-shirts and fabric paint. Suggest that youth define the word *condemnation* on the back of the shirts and then draw a circle around the words, making a slash through the circle signifiying "No Condemnation." Students may think of additional ideas, but encourage them to boldly proclaim the freedom they know in Christ.

Closing: Sing the song "And Can It Be" once more or, as a closing prayer, read aloud together the final verse of the hymn.

Christ Whose Glory Fills the Skies

by Mark Roach

I've always loved metaphors, and Charles Wesley delivers a compelling one in the poetry of this hymn written early in his ministry. He penned the lyrics in 1740, just a few years after he wrote his first known hymn in 1737. I find this most interesting because he himself pointed to the year 1738 as the era of his conversion. These words were written with the zeal of a man who, only two years prior, had endured serious illness and during which time he gave his life to Christ.

With a new lease on life, and the fresh passion of a new believer, he exudes the emotion of a man filled with the Holy Spirit. Wesley pulls the familiar metaphor from **Malachi 4:2**, calling Christ the "Sun of Righteousness," and carries it throughout this hymn. From the very first line he proclaims that Christ's "glory fills the skies," as the sun illuminates everything around us. In the opening stanza he goes on to say that Christ "triumphs o'er the shades of night" and asks Christ to allow his pervasive, powerful light to shine in the worshiper's heart.

Following a true songwriter's tendency, Wesley takes an entirely new angle in the next verse. He now emphasizes the darkness that exists in the absence of the Sun (Christ), utilizing words like "joyless" and "cheerless." I don't know

about you, but in this lyric I get the vision of waking up in a cold, dark room after a stormy night. The window coverings are closed, and I'm not excited about what the day will bring. Then, with a sudden motion, I pull open the curtains and discover the warm glow and radiant beams of the sun, which light up the room in a way that only natural light can.

Finally Wesley brings the metaphor full circle and focuses on the theological implications of the Sun on his life. He declares the power Christ has to "pierce the gloom of sin and grief." He also emphasizes his desire to become increasingly Christlike. Again, from the heart of a new believer, comes the clear longing to grow in faith. This theme is pervasive with lines like "visit then this soul of mine," "fill me, Radiancy divine," and "scatter all my unbelief." Wesley then asks Christ to be increasingly present in his life, until the "perfect day" arrives—a declaration of his intent to live life in a constant effort to become more and more Christlike.

Arguably, no single individual has made the kind of contribution to the music of the Christian church than did Charles Wesley. Writer of thousands of hymns, his work is an absolute staple in our faith and worship today. As a songwriter, it's a joy to study and learn from his lyrical prowess; as a worshiper, it's a joy to lift his writings to my Creator in the form of singing. My hope is that, as you digest these lyrics, you are reminded of the truly pervasive, all-encompassing, and overwhelming nature of the glory of God.

To hear more of Mark's music, visit www.markroach.com.

Worship Meditation: Christ Whose Glory Fills the Skies

Scripture: *"But for you who revere my name the sun of righteousness shall rise, with healing in its wings"* (Malachi 4:2a).

Opening Prayer: "Christ, fill the skies and our lives with your glory. Stay near us and let us always feel your presence. Amen."

Read the Scripture: To help everyone in your group memorize **Malachi 4:2a**, ask each person to read aloud the verse. After everyone has read individually, lead youth to recite the verse together.

Creative Worship: Sing together or listen to "Christ Whose Glory Fills the Skies" from the *Love Divine* CD. This hymn feels more like a poem than a song. Hand out paper and pencils and invite students to rewrite the poem using their own words. Encourage them to be creative and to write the poem as a prayer, and remind them that the phrases do not have to rhyme. After a few minutes, ask for volunteers to read aloud their poems. Encourage youth who are hesitant to be brave.

Closing: Pray a closing prayer, once again asking Christ to shine in your lives like the sun.

Jesus Lover of My Soul

by Chris Eaton

Floods of childhood memories came rushing back to me as I began to read this marvelous Wesley text—laptop poised, musical juices eager to flow! How this Englishman in Nashville has weathered the storms since those frilly, ruffle-adorned, rosy-cheeked choir boy days! Week upon week I would sing high-church music of great beauty and integrity, very little of which stuck between my ears, and even less in my heart. However, that was then and this is now. A softened, broken, redeemed, and grateful heart now beats within me. I am a far different man, yet with just as much enthusiasm for life, love, and other mysteries as that cheeky, ever-singing youth from middle England.

I knew Charles Wesley hymns pretty well—the rousing ones like "And Can It Be" and "I Know That My Redeemer Lives." These songs were fun to sing! Not so with "Jesus Lover of My Soul." Although I knew this particular hymn, the tune made me feel depressed. It sounded like a dirge to my twelve-year-old ears! So here I am, a lifetime later, glued helplessly to the lyrics that embrace my true feelings. The first verse begins, "Jesus, Lover of My Soul, let me to thy bosom fly." How many times have I been flailing in my own torrential storms, desperate to rest my head beneath my mother's arm and return to my ultimate comfort zone.

I am on a journey. We all are. My praise for an awesome God wells up inside me through this hymn. I know God alone can help me. I raise the melody in hope as I sing, "All my trust on thee is stayed, all my help from thee I bring." I am incredibly vulnerable while saying, "Cover my defenseless head with the shadow of thy wing." I still plead, unaware of God's certainty to respond. In the next verse, I'm sinking, fainting, falling deeply, and passionately reaching out for Jesus—"hoping against hope I stand dying and behold I live!" What amazing, incredible news: As I die to myself, I am truly alive in Christ.

The next verse begins with a powerful statement. Certain of my life, I am eager to receive all Christ has for me, proclaiming, "Thou O Christ, art all I want, more than all in thee I find." Surely we all are in the same boat, and the significance of this saving sacrifice is massive. I am overwhelmed. In praise I lift my soul, singing, "Just and holy is thy name." The music thunders in response to truth, "I am all unrighteousness; false and full of sin I am; thou art full of truth and grace"—enough to cover even me!

Through Wesley's words I'm reminded what a glorious Savior we have! The song soars in epic proportions as I sing "thou of life the fountain art." I physically feel the rush of the Holy Spirit completing me in this moment, filling me to overflowing. By some inexplicable miracle, I am taken to the feet of a loving sovereign God, even as I rise to all eternity. Yes, this is a

moment—but also a timeless truth. My path of salvation has been laid before me. It is secured; no matter what I do with my life, I cannot alter it. Jesus, the Son of God, came to earth, died, and was raised to glorious life so that I might be forgiven and my sin covered forever. I cannot take it in. And I do not have to take it in. I only have to faithfully live in God's love and take this great love—fervently, humbly, lovingly—to every hurting soul along life's way.

It is my great hope that you will find, as I have, your unique moment of salvation or renewal as you experience the crashing waves of God's endless grace revealed in these ancient Wesley lyrics. I pray that my melodies, though only a pale reflection of God's amazing beauty, will help you unlock your soul and marvel with me at our inheritance. We are loved—truly and forever. May God richly bless you and keep you ever close.

To hear more of Chris's music, visit www.chriseaton.com.

Worship Meditation: Jesus Lover of My Soul

Scripture: *"In you, O LORD, I take refuge; let me never be put to shame. In your righteousness deliver me and rescue me; incline your ear to me and save me. Be to me a rock of refuge, a strong fortress, to save me, for you are my rock and my fortress" (Psalm 71:1-3).*

Opening Prayer: "Lord, when storms rage all around us, let us find our rest in the shadow of your wings. Remind us that your love can be trusted when the whole world feels like shifting sand. Amen."

Read the Scripture: Ask someone to read aloud **Psalm 71:1-3**.

Creative Worship: Sing together or listen to "Jesus Lover of My Soul" from the *Love Divine* CD. Then invite students to create a physical place of refuge in your meeting space or youth room. Encourage them to make this a space where they can pray or sit in silence and listen for the voice of God—especially during times when storms are raging all around. Provide a supply of candles, Bibles, devotional books, and posters. If trustees allow, even provide paint for the walls. As youth are creating their space, set a tone of worship and prayer by playing background music.

Closing: Pray for God to be your strength.

Jesus the Name High Over All

by Shaun Groves

"What made the communists leave?" I asked.

"God," she said, and broke into a knee-slapping fit of laughter.

It was the same answer I'd heard from the dozen other Ethiopians I'd asked.

"Yes," I responded, after waiting for her giggles to die down. "I know God did it, but what did God use to do it? Was it a failing economy? an armed mob? intervention from another powerful nation? What actually happened to make them pack up and leave your country?"

"God. Did. It." she said. And then she laughed at me some more and told me a story:

When she was nineteen, she said, she was a student at the university in town. One day she courageously spoke to a friend about how she'd just discovered Jesus. Her friend told another. And that friend told another. And before long the authorities threw this young woman in jail. The jail was full of men—debtors, rapists, thieves—the sort of unsavory bunch you'd expect. Luckily she wasn't in her cell very long before they interrogated her. They spat atheist sermons at her, played communist anthems from a dusty cassette deck, beat her, and demanded that she renounce Jesus.

She refused. She refused—and then she preached. She preached Jesus, the King of all kings, the Name over all names, the One who came to break the prisoner's chains. The other inmates watched as she was beaten again. And then she preached again. And was beaten again. And preached again. And as they watched, her courage began to also fill them. Once afraid of their captors, these men began to walk from their shadowed corners and pledge their allegiance to Jesus.

"And that's why the communists left our country," she said, as she laughed again. And this time I laughed with her.

For the first three hundred or so years of Christianity, churches were barracks packed with revolutionaries like this woman, seditionists transferring their allegiance from the principalities and powers of this world to the Name high over all. In those days a convert to The Way would stand before the congregation, raise her hand, and pledge loyalty to God. She knew that by professing her allegiance to Christ, and not to the emperor and his gods, she risked being imprisoned or executed.

"Jesus is Lord!" she would announce. Lord. King. Ruler. Not just over sin and hell but over her fears and failings, her time and talent, her cash and kids, her tongue and thoughts—her everything. All to Jesus she'd surrender, because he's the Name over all.

There's something powerful about this kind of fearless proclamation of devotion—when we mean it. And I don't claim to fully understand how it works to change the world. And I sure can't get a step-by-step answer from the proclaimers I've met. I just know their proclamations change things.

We've seen them chase communists from their palaces in Ethiopia. We've seen them turn fishermen into fishers of men, persecutors into pastors, the blood of martyrs into the bricks of cathedrals. The world watched as this kind of fearless proclamation began a revolution in London during the eighteenth century. Two brothers named Wesley and their friends from school announced to the dutiful Anglicans that God cared more about where their hearts were all week than where their backsides were on Sunday morning. And these changes have changed me.

These days my job is traveling around America, mostly to churches, singing and teaching that Jesus is the name over all—everything. I ask fellow Christians to join me in doing God's will in the third world as it's done in heaven, and I offer suggestions on how we might do that together. The message can be a challenge to deliver. Have you visited a church in America lately? Have you heard the weaselly proclamations we make in these holy places?

"Jesus, you're the Name over all and I know I have enough cash to feed them, but I've been just dying to buy . . . "

"Jesus, you're the Name over all, but this music and that preacher and those pews and, wow, the service is so long; so if you don't mind I think I'd rather . . ."

Imagine if the Wesley brothers had been so cunningly noncommittal in their pledges to God. Imagine if that nineteen-year-old girl had voiced such selfish surrender. Imagine it. Would she have been arrested? Would anyone have believed her a threat? Would Charles and John and their buddies have added to the Anglican church's vertical (toward God) reverence a horizontal (toward others) compassion?

In the hymn "Jesus the Name High Over All," Charles Wesley inspires us to surrender to the God who has broken our fetters and bruised the head of our enemy. Then he shows us what that surrendered life looks like. It's fearless. Power has been spoken into our weak places and life into the dead. It's a life spent announcing the truth of God, regardless of the foes that come against us. And it's a life marked by love so abandoned and so wooing that it pulls cowards from their corners and gives them the strength to stand and shout fearless proclamations of their own.

God does this. We stand—grateful, free, allegiant—and proclaim. And the revolution continues.

To hear more of Shaun's music, visit www.shaungroves.com.

Worship Meditation: Jesus the Name High Over All

Scripture: *"Therefore God also highly exalted him and gave him the name that is above every name"* (Philippians 2:9).

Opening Prayer: "Jesus, you are the name high over all other things in our lives. Remind us to lift our eyes to you and to know that you have your eyes on us. Help us to remember that making you number one in our lives means surrendering all that we have and all that we are to live as your disciples. Amen."

Read the Scripture: Ask a student to read aloud **Philippians 2:9**.

Creative Worship: Hang a large sheet of paper on a wall in the meeting space and set out paints or markers. Ask a student to write the word *Jesus* in large letters across the top of the paper. Then ask students to think of things that crowd out Jesus as the top priority in their lives. Play or sing together "Jesus the Name High Over All" from the *Love Divine* CD. Play some background music to set a prayerful tone while students write under the word *Jesus* the things, situations, and activities that steal Jesus' place as top priority in their lives.

Closing: Gather youth in a circle and holds hands for a closing prayer.

Praise the Lord Who Reigns Above

by Kelly Minter

When I pour over the words of Charles Wesley, I am moved by his many strengths: scriptural knowledge, poetic skill, doctrinal understanding, a heart of worship, and lyrical structure. They are all seamlessly present. "Praise the Lord Who Reigns Above" is no exception, weaving doctrine, poetry, and simplicity of message to praise God—all with a few brilliantly chosen words.

This hymn reminds us of the immeasurable value of a song whose sole attempt is to bring praise to God. In an age when so many of our worship songs are driven by personal pleas for deliverance and comfort, there is refreshing beauty to a lyric that moves aside all daily cares for the joy of focusing exclusively on the greatness of God.

Of course there is great benefit to psalm-like cries in our worship, and, in fact, such songs are desperately needed. But we should never forget the discipline and necessity of directing our eyes upward for the exclusive purpose of exalting our great God.

Perhaps inspired by **Psalm 150**, Charles Wesley's heart behind the lyric seems singularly focused—for God's people to bring God praise. Although the intent seems simple in nature, the doctrine and theology from which Wesley pulls and the poetic nature in which he

weaves together these truths, is a brilliance to behold. Sprinkling the listener with rich and sound doctrine, Wesley uses these truths to elicit a heart of worship, continually circling back to the song's theme: praise to God. Such effective writing subtly drives the point that theological truths were never meant to be confined to the intellect but were always meant to bring us into intimate adoration of God.

I am inspired by Wesley's approach in this song and humbled by his opening line, "Praise the Lord who reigns above and keeps his court below." Gracefully he begins by positioning God as the One who reigns supreme and we, God's people, as the ones under God's reign. Wesley allows us to take our humble places as children, esteeming God as the One who not only rules in heaven but also on earth. For me this comes as a relief, a call to emerge from my self-centeredness and recognize God's sovereignty.

The stanza continues, "Praise the Holy God of love and all his greatness show," juxtaposing God's awe-inspiring holiness with the nature of God's comfort-giving love. Adding to these different but complimentary dimensions, Wesley reminds us of God's vast greatness, calling us to proclaim or "show" it, presumably to a groaning world that is longing for the hope that lies within us. Wesley's words admonish us to praise God for the noble deeds God performs and the power which has no equal. Again I am momentarily freed from my own weakness and frailty as I ponder the unrivaled power and nobility of God.

Beautifully strung into these divine attributes is the inspiring theme that everything good has been born of God. There is nothing good that did not come from God. This is reminiscent of **James 1:17**: "Every generous act of giving, with every perfect gift, is from above, coming down from the Father of lights." Again we see biblical concepts written into this hymn for the purpose of eliciting a heart of praise; we behold wonderful truths in song, allowing us to sing our deepest thanks that, indeed, all good things come from God. In response to God's holiness, greatness, supremacy, and goodness, both Wesley and **Psalm 150** leave no lesser response than for both heaven and earth to adore our God.

The hymn continues to prove rich in theology as the beginning of the final stanza says, "God, in whom they move and live, let every creature sing, glory to their Maker give, and homage to their King." In an economy of words, Wesley draws from another profound truth in **Acts 17:28**, "For 'in him we live and move and have our being.'" Wesley's use of this concept instructs us that it is only in God that any of us share in the grace of life; our lives could not exist apart from God. Because of this blessing, God urges us to bring praise to our Maker and King.

Charles Wesley's vast knowledge of Scripture reveals itself further in the words, "Hallowed be thy name beneath, as in heaven on earth adored." Mined from the Lord's Prayer in **Matthew 6:9-10**, he underscores a

significant plea—that the Lord's name would be hallowed on earth as it is in heaven and that he would be adored on earth as he is in heaven. The imagery and meaning of these words is staggering: Imagine believers on this fallen earth hallowing and adoring the Lord to the extent that he is magnified in heaven. Our worship services would surely be transformed if such an approach were taken. Therein both Scripture and Wesley give us a worthy goal.

"Praise the Lord in every breath, let all things praise the Lord," aptly closes the song, mirroring the final line of the Book of Psalms, "Let everything that breathes praise the LORD! Praise the LORD!" (**Psalm 150:6**). In response to God's supremacy, reign, holiness, love, greatness, power, nobility, and goodness, we are left with no higher calling or privilege in life than to praise our Sustainer. In honor of Charles Wesley, we sing his songs to praise the Lord who reigns above, knowing that this is the grandest celebration of a life such as his.

To hear more of Kelly's music, visit www.kellyminter.com.

Worship Meditation: Praise the Lord Who Reigns Above

Scripture: *"Praise the LORD! Praise God in his sanctuary; praise him in his mighty firmament! (Psalm 150:1).*

Opening Prayer: "Lord, we praise you for your amazing creation, your awesome deeds, and your unfailing love. Hear our praise as we turn our hearts to you. Amen."

Read the Scripture: Begin by asking one youth to read aloud the first verse of **Psalm 150**. Then ask another youth to begin reading the second verse, continuing until the last verse has been read.

Creative Worship: Collect a variety of hand drums. (Try to collect enough drums for each student to have one drum to play. You may need to supplement by collecting other percussion instruments.) Play the song "Praise the Lord Who Reigns Above" from the *Love Divine* CD. Allow youth to play their drums as a prayer of praise. Encourage them to have fun as they worship their Creator.

Closing: Read **Psalm 150** aloud together to declare your praise to God.

O For a Heart to Praise My God

by Jenny Youngman

Truthfully I had never heard of this great Wesley hymn until I was preparing to write this reflection. I've got my favorites, and even a basic retention of several first lines, but this hymn had escaped my memory. Charles Wesley had such a sense of poetry that he could translate our hearts' deepest desires and articulate them into such beautiful, singable language.

When I listen to these lyrics, I find myself recalling **Psalm 139**. The psalmist wrote, "Search me, O God, and know my heart; test me and know my thoughts. See if there is any wicked way in me, and lead me in the way everlasting" (verses 23–24). I hear Wesley in deep, poetic prayer for a heart that is humble, hopeful, open, and faithful—"a humble, lowly contrite heart, believing, true, and clean."

What is the state of your heart? Is it tuned and ready to praise God? Is it humble, contrite, and ready to receive? My prayer for you as you live with this great Wesley hymn, is that you would open your ears to a beautiful new melody and open your heart to ancient words that fill your heart with love divine.

To hear Jenny's music, visit
www.jennyyoungman.com.

Worship Meditation: O For a Heart to Praise My God

Scripture: *"Search me, O God, and know my heart; test me and know my thoughts. See if there is any wicked way in me, and lead me in the way everlasting"* (Psalm 139:23-24).

Opening Prayer: "God, we pray that you would open our hearts, that you would make us humble and soft like clay for you to shape and mold. Search out the sin and impurities—anything that keeps us from living all-out for you. Lead us to your heart. Amen."

Read the Scripture: Encourage your youth to memorize **Psalm 139:23-24.** Spend a few minutes reciting the verses together, then move around the room and ask each person to say them aloud. After everyone has recited the verse, shout it out together once and then whisper it once. Hopefully that will be the beginning of your youth internalizing the text.

Creative Worship: To set a prayerful mood, play or sing the song, "O For a Heart to Praise My God" from the *Love Divine* CD. Give each student a portion of modeling clay, along with instructions to knead the clay until it is soft. Then ask youth to create symbols of opening their hearts to God (for example, the shape of a heart, a flower bud opening, or even an "O" for "Open").

Closing: Invite those who wish to tell about their creations, then close in prayer.

Jesus We Look to Thee

by Jenny Youngman

To what or to whom are you looking? Are you looking for the presence of Christ in your life? Where have you seen the work of God in your life this week? this month? this year?

In the hymn "Jesus We Look to Thee," Charles Wesley declares that we will keep our eyes open to notice the ways in which the Spirit of God moves in and around us. God is always present and working in us. The question is are we looking?

My favorite line in this hymn is, "Present we know thou art, but O thyself reveal." How many times have you said with your mouth that you know God is always with you, then with the same mouth wondered where God is? We believe and trust God's Word that the Spirit is always present with us. And sometimes just knowing that God is present is enough for us. But most times it's a revelation that we need: "O thyself reveal." Show us, God, where you are and what you're doing in us.

This hymn reminds us of God's presence and revelation in our lives. So I ask again: "Where have you seen God working in your life? Are you looking?"

Worship Meditation: Jesus We Look to Thee

Scripture: *"If you love me, you will keep my commandments. And I will ask the Father, and he will give you another Advocate, to be with you forever. . . . You will know him, because he abides with you, and he will be in you"* (John 14:15-17).

Opening Prayer: "Lord, we know that you are always with us, but sometimes we need a tangible sign. We pray for dramatic revelation—something to really grab our attention. Make our ears and hearts attentive to your presence and help us to keep our eyes open to see you. Amen."

Read the Scripture: Ask three readers to read aloud one verse each of **John 14:15-17**.

Creative Worship: Sing together the song, "Jesus We Look to Thee" from the *Love Divine* CD. Then give each student a pocket-sized notebook and a pen. Suggest they find a quiet space to journal or doodle as they reflect on the presence of God in their lives. Ask the question, "Where do you see God in your life?" Allow youth an extended period of time to pray through this question using their journals.

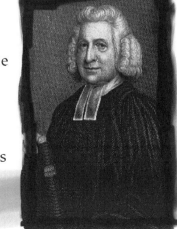

Closing: Come back together as a group and sing the hymn once more as a closing prayer.

Rejoice the Lord Is King

by Jenny Youngman

Charles Wesley knew how to get a crowd rejoicing and declaring their love for God. "Rejoice the Lord Is King" reads almost like a national anthem with phrases like "Jesus the Savior reigns" and "his kingdom cannot fail." This is a song for Jesus-followers to sing at full blast with hands raised, proclaiming that the God we serve is Lord of our lives, and this Lord cannot fail! This Lord is One worth serving!

Wesley paints a picture of the Kingdom reign on earth and the eternal reign of God. Just as we can trust in God's unfailing love on earth, we can trust in the unfailing promise of life in heaven with God. Nothing on earth can diminish the power of God in our lives— no sin, no idol, no circumstance. Jesus the Savior reigns!

When you feel like you have no advocate . . . when you feel like no one is on your side . . . when you feel like you've made too many mistakes . . . when you feel like the world is against you: Rejoice! The Lord is King! He is the God of truth and love. Triumph evermore! Be at peace. Jesus is our King today and for all eternity. Lift up your heart and lift up your voice.

Rejoice! God is with you!

Worship Meditation: Rejoice the Lord Is King

Scripture: *"Rejoice in the Lord always; again I will say, Rejoice. Let your gentleness be known to everyone. The Lord is near. Do not worry about anything, but in everything by prayer and supplication with thanksgiving let your requests be made known to God. And the peace of God, which surpasses all understanding, will guard your hearts and your minds in Christ Jesus"* (Philippians 4:4-7).

Opening Prayer: "Lord, we rejoice in the hope that we have in you. We rejoice that you have conquered sin and death. We rejoice that you are always near. We rejoice that we need not worry but only turn to you. Hear our praise. Amen."

Read the Scripture: Lead youth in reading aloud together **Philippians 4:4-7**.

Creative Worship: Ask your student musicians to learn and lead the group in singing "Rejoice the Lord Is King" from the *Love Divine* CD. Then hand out magazines, newspapers, glue, and scissors. Ask the students to create a collage that represents Jesus as the King of their lives. Play background music as they work.

Closing: Call on volunteers to show and talk about their collages, then close in prayer, rejoicing in God your Savior.

Attend strictly to the
sense of what you sing,
and see that your heart
is not carried away
with the sound,
but offered to God
continually.

Songs

And Can It Be

Verse 1

| D   G |D |D   G |D

|D   G |D |D   G |D

And can it be that I should gain an interest in the Savior's blood!

|D   A |Bm, |G   Em |A

Died he for me? who caused His pain! For me? who Him to death pursued?

|G |D |D |A

Amazing love! How can it be that thou, my God, shouldst die for me?

|G |Bm |D   A |D G |D

Amazing love! How can it be that thou, my God, shouldst die for me?

Verse 2

|D   G |D |D   G |D

'Tis mystery all: the Immortal dies! Who can explore his strange design?

|D   A |Bm, |G   Em |A

In vain the first-born seraph tries to sound the depths of love divine.

|G |D |D |A

'Tis mercy all! Let earth adore; let angel minds inquire no more.

|G |Bm |D   A |D   G |D

'Tis mercy all! Let earth adore; let angel minds inquire no more.

Verse 3

|D   G |D |D G |D

He left His Father's throne above (so free, so infinite His grace!),

|D   A |Bm, |G   Em |A

emptied himself of all but love, and bled for Adam's helpless race.

Words by Charles Wesley
Music by Chris Eaton, John Hartley, and Gareth Robinson

```
  G              D           D              A
'Tis mercy all, immense and free, for O my God, it found out me!

  G              Bm          D     A     D     G   D
'Tis mercy all, immense and free, for O my God, it found out me!
```

Verse 4
```
        D     G   D              D     G     D
Long my imprisoned spirit lay, fast bound in sin and nature's night;

       D     A    Bm,          G     Em        A
thine eye diffused a quickening ray; I woke, the dungeon flamed with light;

     G              D              D              A
my chains fell off, my heart was free, I rose, went forth, and followed thee.

     G              Bm             D      A     D   G D
My chains fell off, my heart was free, I rose, went forth, and followed thee.
```

Verse 5
```
        D     G   D              D     G     D
No condemnation now I dread; Jesus, and all in him, is mine;

     D     A    Bm,            G     Em   A
alive in him, my living Head, and clothed in righteousness divine,

     G              D              D                  A
bold I approach the eternal throne, and claim the crown, through Christ my own

     G              Bm             D          A     D
Bold I approach the eternal throne, and claim the crown, through Christ my own

     G              Bm             D          A     D   G D
Bold I approach the eternal throne, and claim the crown, through Christ my own.
```

D   G   A   Bm   Em

Come Thou Long Expected Jesus

Verse 1

D | D | D | D   A |
Come, thou long-expected Jesus, born to set thy people free;

D | D | D | A   D |
from our fears and sins release us, let us find our rest in thee.

G   D | A   Bm | G   D | A |
Israel's strength and consolation, hope of all the earth thou art;

Bm | G   D | D   G   A | D |
dear desire of every nation, joy of every longing heart.

Verse 2

D | D | D | D   A |
Born thy people to deliver, born a child and yet a King,

D | D | D | A   D |
born to reign in us forever, now thy gracious kingdom bring.

G   D | A   Bm | G   D | A |
By thine own eternal spirit rule in all our hearts alone;

Bm | G   D | D   G   A | D |
by thine all sufficient merit, raise us to thy glorious throne.

Chorus

| A | D | G   D | A   A | Bm | G | D
Rejoice! Rejoice! Immanuel. Rejoice! Rejoice! Glory be to God.

G | G | D |
Glory be to God in the highest.

Words by Charles Wesley
Music by Chris Eaton, John Hartley, and Gareth Robinson

D	A	G	Bm	Em
xx0	x0 0	000	x x	0 000
132	123	21 3	1342	12

I Know That My Redeemer Lives

Verse 1

C		C	F		G		F	G		C		C

I know that my Redeemer lives, and ever prays for me.

C	C	F	G	F	G	C		C

A token of his love he gives, a pledge of liberty.

Verse 2

C	C	F	G	F	G	C		C

Jesus, I hang on every word I steadfastly believe.

C	C	F	G	F	G	C		C

You will return and claim me, Lord, and to yourself receive.

Chorus

F	G	Am	Am

And we lift you up, Hallelujah, Holy is our God.

F	G	Am	Am

And we will worship you and honor your name.

F	G	Am	Am

Worthy is the Lamb, Hallelujah, you reign in majesty.

F	G	C	F

Glory to our God, forever the same.

Words by Charles Wesley
Music by Chris Eaton and John Hartley

Verse 3

| C | C | | F | G | | F | | G | C | | C |

Joyful in hope, my spirit soars to meet you from above.

| C | | C | | F | G | | F | | G | | C | | C |

Your goodness thankfully adores, and sure, I taste your love.

Repeat Chorus

Verse 4

| C | C | | F | | G | | F | G | | C | | C |

Your love I soon expect to find in all its depth and height;

| C | | C | | F | | G | | F | | G | C | | C |

to comprehend the eternal mind and grasp the infinite.

Repeat Chorus twice

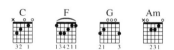

Jesus Lover of My Soul

Verse 1

Am   Am   E   E

Jesus, lover of my soul, let me to thy bosom fly,

Am   Am   E   E

while the nearer waters roll, while the tempest still is high.

F   F   Am   Am

Hide me, O my Savior, hide, till the storm of life is past;

E   E   F   G   Am   F

Safe into the haven guide; O receive my soul at last.

Verse 2

Am   Am   E   E

Other refuge have I none, hangs my helpless soul on Thee.

Am   Am   E   E

Leave, ah! leave me not alone; still support and comfort me.

F   F   C   C

All my trust on thee is stayed, all my help from thee I bring.

G   G   F   E   A   F

cover my defenseless head with the shadow of thy wing.

Verse 3

Am   Am   E   E

Wilt thou not regard my call? Wilt thou not accept my prayer.

Am   Am   E   E

Lo, I sink, I faint, I fall. Lo, on thee I cast my care.

Words by Charles Wesley
Music by Chris Eaton and John Hartley

F		F				Am	Am		

F | F | Am | Am

Reach me out thy gracious hand, while I of thy strength receive,

E | E | F | G | Am | F

Hoping against hope I stand, dying and behold I live.

Verse 4

Am | Am | E | E

Thou, O Christ, art all I want, more than all in thee I find;

Am | Am | E | E

raise the fallen, cheer the faint, heal the sick, and lead the blind.

F | F | Am | Am

Just and holy is thy name, I am all unrighteousness;

E | E | F | G | Am | F

false and full of sin I am; thou art full of truth and grace.

Verse 5

F | F | C | C

Plenteous grace with thee is found, grace to cover all my sin;

G | G | F | E

let the healing streams abound, make and keep me pure within.

F | F | C | C

Thou of life the fountain art, freely let me take of thee.

G | G | F | G | Am

Spring Thou up within my heart and rise to all eternity.

Am   E   F   G   C

231   231   134211   21 3   32 1

Jesus the Name High Over All

Verse 1

C   Am   F   C   C   Am   Gsus

Jesus, the name high over all, in hell or earth or sky;

C   Am   F   C   Dm7 Gsus   Csus   C

angels and men before it fall, and devils fear and fly.

C   Am   F   C   C   Am   Gsus

Jesus, the name to sinners dear, the name to sinners given;

C   Am   F   C   Dm7   Gsus Gsus   G

it scatters all their guilty fear, and turns their hell to heaven.

G   C   G   C   F   Gsus   G

O that the world might taste and see the riches of his grace!

C   Am   F   C   Dm7 Gsus   F

The arms of love that compass me would all the world embrace.

Verse 2

C   Am   F   C   C   Am   Gsus

Jesus, the prisoner's fetters breaks and bruises Satan's head.

C   Am   F   C   Dm7 Gsus Csus   C

Power into strengthless souls it speaks, and life into the dead.

G   C   G   C   F   Gsus   G

Thee I shall constantly proclaim, though earth and hell oppose;

C   Am   F   C   Dm7 Gsus   F

bold to confess thy glorious name before a world of foes.

Words by Charles Wesley
Music by Chris Eaton, John Hartley, and Gareth Robinson

Verse 3

```
C        Am      ¦F   C   ¦C        Am     ¦Gsus            ¦
His only righteousness I show, his saving truth proclaim;


C        Am      ¦F   C  ¦Dm7     Gsus    ¦Csus    C   ¦
'tis all my business here below to cry "Behold the Lamb."


G      C      ¦G   C     ¦F              ¦Gsus     G   ¦
Happy, if with my latest breath, I may but gasp his name,


C           Am    ¦F  C       ¦Dm7    Gsus  ¦C              ¦
preach him to all and cry in death, "Behold, behold the Lamb!"
```

Jesus We Look to Thee

Verse 1

D   D   G   D
Jesus, we look to thee,   thy promised presence claim.

D   Bm7   G   A
Thou in the midst of us   shall be assembled in thy name.

  Gmaj7   D   F♯   Bm7
Thy name, salvation is, which we here come to prove;

  G   G   A   D   G   A   Gmaj7   A
Thy name is life and health and peace and everlasting love.

Verse 2

D   D   G   D
Not in the name of pride   or selfishness we meet.

D   Bm7   G   A
From nature's paths we turn aside   and worldly thoughts forget.

  Gmaj7   D   F♯   Bm7
We meet thy grace to take which thou hast freely given.

  G   G   A   D   G   A   Gmaj7   A
We meet on earth for thy dear sake that we may meet in heaven.

Words by Charles Wesley
Music by Chris Eaton and John Hartley

Verse 3

D   D   G   D
Present we know thou art,   but, O, thyself, reveal.

D   Bm7   G   A
Now, Lord, let every waiting heart the mighty comfort feel.

Gmaj7   D   F#   Bm7
O may thy quickening voice the sin of death remove,

G   G   A D   G   A   Gmaj7   A
And bid our inmost souls rejoice in hope of perfect love.

D   G   Bm7   Gmaj7   F#   A

Love Divine All Loves Excelling

Verse 1

    C   C   F   C
Love divine, all loves excelling, joy of heaven to earth come down;

    G   Am   F   C   G C   F
fix in us thy humble dwelling; all thy faithful mercies crown!

    C   C   F   C
Jesus, thou art all compassion, pure, unbounded love thou art;

    G   Am   F   C   G C
visit us with thy salvation; enter every trembling heart.

Verse 2

    Gm   Dm   F   C
Come, Almighty to deliver, let us all thy life receive;

    Gm   F   Dm   F
suddenly return and never, nevermore thy temples leave.

G7sus4 C   C   F   Em
Thee we would be always blessing, serve thee as thy hosts above;

    Am   G   F   F Am C   F   C   C   Dm
pray and praise thee without ceasing, glory in thy perfect love.

Words by Charles Wesley
Music by Chris Eaton and John Hartley

Verse 3

     Gm   Dm   F   C

Finish, then, thy new creation; pure and spotless let us be.

     Gm   F   Dm   F

Let us see Thy great salvation perfectly restored in thee;

G7sus4   C   C   F   Em

changed from glory into glory, till in heaven we take our place,

     Am G F   F Am C   F   C   C

till we cast our crowns before thee, lost in wonder, love, and praise.

C   F   G   Am   Gm   Dm   G7sus4   Em   D

Praise the Lord Who Reigns Above

Verse 1

D   G   D   G

Praise the Lord who reigns above and keeps his court below;

G   G   D A D

praise the holy God of love and all his greatness show;

D   G   D   A

praise him for his noble deeds, praise him for his matchless power;

Bm   G   G A   D

him from whom all good proceeds let earth and heaven adore,

  G A D   G

let earth and heaven adore.

Chorus

    D G   D A

Praise the name of Christ; celebrate and lift him up high.

    Bm D G G   A G A

Praise the Lord of life. We'll sing the story of honor and glory

  G   A D   G

and praise the name of Christ.

Verse 2

D   G   D   G

God, in whom they move and live, let every creature sing,

Words by Charles Wesley
Music by Chris Eaton and John Hartley

```
G          G          D     A    D
```
glory to their maker give, and homage to their King.

```
D          G          D          A
```
Hallowed be thy name beneath, as in heaven on earth adored.

```
Bm         G          G     A    D
```
praise the Lord in every breath, let all things praise the Lord;

```
   G     A      D      G
```
let all things praise the Lord.

Repeat Chorus

Bridge
```
G  A G A  G A G A  G  A G A
```
Hallelujah, hallelujah, hallelujah.

```
G          A     G     A    G       A
```
We'll sing the story of honor and glory and praise the name.

Repeat Chorus twice

Rejoice the Lord Is King

Verse 1

| C | F | G | C |

Rejoice, the Lord is King! Your Lord and King adore;

| C | F | D | G |

mortals, give thanks and sing, and triumph evermore.

| C | F | F | Am | Am |

Lift up your heart,   lift up your voice;

| Em | F   G | C | Bb | F | Eb |

rejoice; again I say, rejoice.

Verse 2

| C | F | G | C |

Jesus the Savior reigns, the God of truth and love;

| C | F | D | G |

when he had purged our stains, he took his seat above.

| C | F | F | Am | Am |

Lift up your heart,   lift up your voice;

| Em | F   G | C | C |

rejoice; again I say, rejoice.

Verse 3

| E | E | Am | Am |

His kingdom cannot fail; he rules o'er earth and heaven;

Words by Charles Wesley
Music by Chris Eaton, John Hartley, and Gareth Robinson

```
   D              D    G         G
the keys of death and hell are to our Jesus given.


   E             E    Am        Am
He sits at God's right hand; till all his foes submit;


   D             D    G         G
and bow to his command and fall beneath his feet.


   C      F    F          Am       Am
Lift up your heart,    lift up your voice;


 Em   F   G  C        Bb       F       Eb
rejoice; again I say, rejoice.
```

Verse 4
```
 C             F    G             C
Rejoice in glorious hope! Jesus the Judge shall come,


 C             F    D         G
and take his servants up to their eternal home.


   C       F   F          Am      Am
We soon shall hear    th'archangel's voice;


 Em    F      G      C
the trump of God shall sound, rejoice!


 F    G   C    F    G   C
Again, I say rejoice; again, I say rejoice.
```

C F G D Am Em Bb Eb E

O For a Thousand Tongues

Verse 1

G   Gmaj7   C   G   D
O for a thousand tongues to sing my great Redeemer's praise,

Am   Em   C   Em   D   G
the glories of my God and King, the triumphs of his grace!

Verse 2

B   Em   D   G
My gracious Master and my God, assist me to proclaim,

C   Em   C   D   Em
to spread through all the earth abroad the honors of thy name,

C   D   G
the honors of thy name.

Verse 3

G   Gmaj7   C   G   D
Jesus! the name that charms our fears, that bids our sorrows cease;

Am   Em   C   Em   D   G
'tis music in the sinner's ears, 'tis life, and health, and peace.

Verse 4

B   Em   D   G
He breaks the power of canceled sin, he sets the prisoner free;

C   Em   C   D   Em
his blood can make the foulest clean; his blood availed for me,

C   D   G   Gmaj7   Em   C
his blood availed for me.

Words by Charles Wesley
Music by Chris Eaton and John Hartley

Verse 5

G   Gmaj7   C   G   D
He speaks, and listening to his voice, new life the dead receive;

   Am   Em   C   Em   D   G
the mournful, broken hearts rejoice, the humble poor believe.

Verse 6

   B   Em   D   G
Hear him, ye deaf; his praise, ye dumb, your loosened tongues employ;

   C   Em   C   D   Em
ye blind, behold your Savior come, and leap, ye lame, for joy,

   C   D   G   Gmaj7   G6   Gmaj7
and leap, ye lame, for joy.

Verse 7

G   Gmaj7   C   G   D
In Christ, your head, you then shall know, shall feel your sins forgiven;

   Am Em   C   Em   D   G
anticipate your heaven below, and own that love is heaven.

Verse 8

   B   Em   D   G
Glory to God in praise and love, be ever ever given.

   C   Em   C   D   Em
By saints below and saints above, the church in earth and heaven,

   C   D   G   Gmaj7   G6   Gmaj7   G
the church in earth and heaven.

G   Gmaj7   C   D   Em   Am   B   G6

Christ Whose Glory Fills the Skies

Verse 1

E   Emaj7 | E6 | E   Emaj7 | E6 B |
Christ, whose glory fills the skies, Christ, the true, the only light,

E   Emaj7 | E6 | A   C#m | B | E |
Sun of Righteousness, arise, triumph o'er the shades of night;

B   E | E   A | A   C#m | B | Emaj7 | Amaj7
Dayspring from on high, be near; Daystar, in my heart appear.

Verse 2

E   Emaj7 | E6 | E   Emaj7| C#m | B |
Dark and cheerless is the morn unaccompanied by thee;

E   Emaj7 | A | A   C#m | B | E |
joyless is the day's return, till thy mercy's beams I see;

B   E | E   A | A   C#m | B | Emaj7 | Amaj7
till they inward light impart, cheer my eyes and warm my heart.

Verse 3

E   Emaj7| E6   E | E   Emaj7 | E6   B |
Visit then this soul of mine; pierce the gloom of sin and grief;

E   Emaj7| A | A   C#m | B | E |
fill me, Radiancy divine, scatter all my unbelief;

B   E | E   A | A C#m | B | E |
more and more thyself display, shining to the perfect day.

B   E | E   A | A C#m | B | Emaj7 | Amaj7 | E |
More and more thyself display, shining to the perfect day.

Words by Charles Wesley
Music by Chris Eaton and John Hartley

Songs

O For a Heart to Praise My God

Verse 1

G | C   G | C   Am | Dsus   D

O for a heart to praise my God, a heart from sin set free,

| C   G | C   Cm6 | G   D | G |

a heart that always feels thy blood so freely shed for me.

Verse 2

G | C   G | C   Am | Dsus   D

A heart resigned, submissive, meek, my great Redeemer's throne,

| C   G | C   Cm6 | G   D | G |

where only Christ is heard to speak, where Jesus reigns alone.

Verse 3

G   C | Am   D | G   C | Dsus   D

A humble, lowly, contrite heart, believing, true, and clean,

| C   G | C   Cm6 | G   D | G |

which neither life nor death can part from Christ who dwells within.

Verse 4

G | C   G | C   Am | Dsus   D

A heart in every thought renewed and full of love divine,

| C   G | C   Cm6 | G   D | G |

perfect and right and pure and good, a copy, Lord, of thine.

Words by Charles Wesley
Music by Chris Eaton, John Hartley, and Gareth Robinson

Verse 5

```
G                    ¦C      G     ¦C      Am  ¦Dsus    D
```
Thy nature, gracious Lord, impart; come quickly from above;

```
       ¦C      G    ¦C    Cm6    ¦G       D    ¦G
```
write thy new name upon my heart, thy new, best name of Love.

```
       ¦C      G    ¦C    Cm6    ¦          D    ¦G
```
Write thy new name upon my heart, thy new, best name of Love.

Worship Feast Resources

The WORSHIP FEAST series offers practical ways to meet the worship needs of postmodern youth and young adults and to help them experience God in a new way.

- *Worship Feast Lent and Easter* NEW!
  Offers youth leaders an exciting alternative to other Lent and Easter worship fare.
  Includes seven original Lent-themed worship songs on an audio CD along with printed lyrics and chords.
  ISBN: 9780687643998 (Abingdon Press)

- *Worship Feast Liturgical Dance—8 Easy-to-Learn Dances for Worship* (DVD)
  Features step-by-step instructional choreography for liturgical dance for any skill level.
  ISBN: 9780687643776 (Abingdon Press)

- *Worship Feast Prayer Stations*
  A collection of video instructions of a youth pastor creating and talking about various prayer stations.
  Also includes slide shows and original music.
  ISBN: 9780687493777 (Abingdon Press)

- *Worship Feast Readings—50 Readings, Rituals, Prayers, and Guided Meditations*
  A collection of readings to use in creating meaningful worship, devotion, and prayer times for youth.
  ISBN: 9780687741816 (Abingdon Press)

- *Worship Feast Services—50 Complete Multi-Sensory Services for Youth*
  Includes services for the various seasons, prayer and healing, discovering your spiritual type, graduates, and many more. ISBN: 9780687063673 (Abingdon Press)

- *Worship Feast Ideas—100 Awesome Ideas for Postmodern Youth*
  Ideas for creating your own services or incorporating multisensory worship elements into your existing services, including incense, silence, secular music, and more. ISBN: 9780687063574 (Abingdon Press)

- *Worship Feast Dramas—15 Sketches for Youth Groups, Worship, and More*
  Includes a variety of long and short skits field-tested with youth in real-life situations.
  ISBN: 9780687044597 (Abingdon Press)

- *Worship Feast Taizé—20 Complete Services in the Spirit of Taizé*
  Services offer meditations, song suggestions, prayers, and use of silence. Includes a split-track, instrumental music CD.
  ISBN: 9780687741915 (Abingdon Press)

- *Worship Feast Taizé Songbook*
  Includes 15 popular and easy-to-sing Taizé songs, featuring simple melody lines, guitar chords, and the text in English and other languages.
  ISBN: 9780687739325 (Abingdon Press)

Worship Feast
Charles Wesley

features the album *Love Divine*

Classic Wesley hymns come alive again for a new generation with creative and contemporary music.

Some of today's leading Christian artists perform as worship twelve celebrated hymns of the Christian church. You'll want to have the CD for use with WORSHIP FEAST CHARLES WESLEY. And you'll want to have extra copies for your youth resource library and maybe for your students!

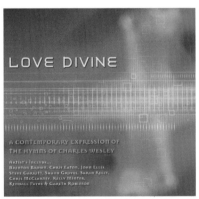

LOVE DIVINE

A CONTEMPORARY EXPRESSION OF
THE HYMNS OF CHARLES WESLEY

ARTISTS INCLUDE...
BRENTON BROWN, CHRIS EATON, JOHN ELLIS,
STEVE GARRETT, SARAH GROVES, SARAH KELLY,
CHRIS McCLARNEY, KELLY MINTER,
KENDALL PAYNE & GARETH ROBINSON

ISBN 5019282282122